PATIENCE

THE BENEFITS
OF
WAITING

6 Studies for Groups or Individuals
With Notes for Leaders

STEPHEN EYRE

ZondervanPublishingHouse
Grand Rapids, Michigan

A Division of HarperCollins*Publishers*

Published by Zondervan Publishing House
Grand Rapids, Michigan 49530

ISBN 0-310-53681-2

Editor: Jack Kuhatschek
Cover design: Tammy Grabrian Johnson
Cover photo: Richard T. Nowitz 1990
Interior design: Rachel Hostetter

Printed in the United States of America
97 98 99 00 / DP / 12 11 10 9

Contents

To our English hosts
Ray, Pam, Sally, Andrew

Fruit of the Spirit Bible Studies

WELCOME TO Fruit of the Spirit Bible Studies. This series was written with one goal in mind—to allow the Spirit of God to use the Word of God to produce his fruit in your life.

To get the most from this series you need to understand a few basic facts:

Fruit of the Spirit Bible Studies are designed to be flexible. You can use them in your quiet times or for group discussion. They are ideal for Sunday-school classes, small groups, or neighborhood Bible studies.

The eight guides in this series can be used in any order that is best for you or your group.

Because each guide contains only six studies, you can easily explore more than one fruit of the Spirit. In a Sunday-school class, any two guides can be combined for a quarter (twelve weeks), or the entire series can be covered in a year.

Each study deliberately focuses on only one or two passages. That allows you to see each passage in its context, avoiding the temptation of prooftexting and the frustration of "Bible hopscotch" (jumping from verse to verse). If you would like to look up additional passages, a Bible concordance will give the most help.

The questions help you *discover* what the Bible says rather than simply *telling* you what it says. They encourage you to think and to explore options rather than to merely fill in the blanks with one-word answers.

Leader's notes are provided in the back of the guide. They show how to lead a group discussion, provide additional information on questions, and suggest ways to deal with problems that may come up in the discussion. With such helps, someone with little or no experience can lead an effective study.

Suggestions for Individual Study

1. Begin each study with prayer. Ask God to help you understand the passage and to apply it to your life.

2. A good modern translation, such as the *New International Version*, the *New American Standard Bible*, or the *Revised Standard Version*, will give you the most help. However, the questions in this guide are based on the *New International Version*.

3. Read and reread the passage(s). You must know what the passage says before you can understand what it means and how it applies to you.

4. Write your answers in the space provided in the study guide. This will help you to clearly express your understanding of the passage.

5. Keep a Bible dictionary handy. Use it to look up any unfamiliar words, names, or places.

Suggestions for Group Study

1. Come to the study prepared. Careful preparation will greatly enrich your time in group discussion.

2. Be willing to join in the discussion. The leader of the group will not be lecturing but will encourage people to discuss what they have learned in the passage. Plan to share what God has taught you in your individual study.

3. Stick to the passage being studied. Base your answers on the verses being discussed rather than on outside authorities such as commentaries or your favorite author or speaker.

4. Try to be sensitive to the other members of the group. Listen attentively when they speak, and be affirming whenever you can. This will encourage more hesitant members of the group to participate.

5. Be careful not to dominate the discussion. By all means participate! But allow others to have equal time.

6. If you are the discussion leader, you will find additional suggestions and helpful ideas in the leader's notes at the back of the guide.

PATIENCE
The Benefits of Waiting

Lᴏʀᴅ, I WANT PATIENCE, and I want it *right now!*"
It is easier to joke about patience than to become patient. You can tell that God is growing patience in you, not when you are patient, but when you run into frustrating experiences; when others fail to meet your expectations; when people you depend on let you down; when the things you depend on keep breaking. Most of all, you know you are learning patience when you call out to the Lord for help, and he seems to be on vacation.

I am not an expert on patience; it doesn't come naturally to me. I am constantly aware that there is more to do than there is time to do it. Frequently, there is a sense of urgency that pushes me from the inside.

There are lots of reasons for this inward push: my inward desire to feel important and productive, and the perceived expectations of family and friends to get things done. Even the commercials on television tell me to hurry if I am to take advantage of the best deal available "today only."

God is not pleased with this sense of hurry. As a result, my life with him has included a lengthy term of schooling in a different way of living. When I say, "Quick," God seems to say, "Slow." When I say "Now," God seems to say, "Later."

In puzzling through these frustrating interactions with God, I have come to see that waiting, and the patience it requires, occupies a central role in Scripture in shaping God's people. God called Abraham and promised him a whole nation of children. Yet during his life Abraham and Sarah only had one son, and they had to wait over twenty-five years for him to be born. Along the way, Abraham had some very wonderful and very painful times with God.

God called David to be the king of Israel. But before David ascended to the throne, he had to live as a fugitive in the desert for ten years while Saul chased him. Even a cursory look at the book of Psalms reveals that David did not enjoy those years. Yet God thought they were important for David and used them to shape David's character.

Learning to wait patiently on God is worth it. The benefits include the ability to influence others in godliness, the certainty of God's blessings, a deeper knowledge of Scripture, a growing patience and forgiveness of others, and a certain hope to sustain us even in the darkest times.

This Fruit of the Spirit guide contains six studies on patience. We will look at The Benefits of Patience, The Blessings of Perseverance, The Virtue of Slowness, Patience & Forgiveness, Waiting for the Lord, and Waiting until the End.

As you work through each of these studies, my prayer is that you will begin to see the fruit of patience ripening in your life.

A patient man has great understanding, but a quick-tempered man displays folly.

Proverbs 14:29

A hot-tempered man stirs up dissension, but a patient man calms a quarrel.

Proverbs 15:18

Better a patient man than a warrior, a man who controls his temper than one who takes a city.

Proverbs 16:32

A man's wisdom gives him patience; it is to his glory to overlook an offense.

Proverbs 19:11

Through patience a ruler can be persuaded, and a gentle ▪tongue can break a bone.

Proverbs 25:15

1

The Benefits of Patience

S<small>TOP IT!"</small>

"No!"

"You are going to break Dad's computer!"

"Its my turn!"

The game of computer monopoly comes to an abrupt halt. My youngest son stomps out of the study and runs upstairs to his room. My two older sons walk away, exasperated. So much for a quiet Sunday afternoon.

With a little more patience the game could have gone on. But the boys were tired, and it was a hot afternoon. Patience on such days is not in great supply.

For most of us, more is at stake during frustrating times than a children's game. Yet it is in the trying times, when we seem least inclined to be patient, that we need it the most. We can be encouraged to grow in patience if we look at its benefits in the book of Proverbs.

1. Take a patience inventory. At what times and in what circumstances do you tend to be impatient?

2. Read the five proverbs listed on page 10. How would you summarize the qualities of a patient person?

3. What contrasts are drawn between a patient and impatient person?

4. Look at Proverbs 15:18. How does patience/impatience affect our relationships with others?

   How have you seen patience/impatience affect relationships in your life?

5. Read Proverbs 16:32. Why do you think a patient person is better than a warrior or one who takes a city?

6. How could patience be a great asset in your (choose one) workplace, classroom, home?

7. Read Proverbs 14:29 and 19:11. How does patience—or the lack of it—reveal whether a person is wise or foolish?

8. Think of a person you know who is very patient. In what other ways does that person seem wise?.

9. Look at Proverbs 15:18 and 25:15. How does patience or impatience affect the impact of our speech?

10. Look again at Proverbs 16:32 and 25:15. What is the difference between patience and passiveness?

What is the difference between patience and powerlessness?

11. What changes do you need to make in the way you act and think in order to become more patient?

12. Ask God to help you grow in patience during the course of these studies.

2

The Blessings of Perseverance

I AM NOT SEEING MUCH FRUIT in my ministry right now. At least not to my satisfaction. Why aren't there more converts? Why aren't there more people in Bible studies? And why aren't there more growing Christians?

Sometimes I think I am in the wrong profession. Maybe I ought to give up and get a "real" job. Then I remind myself that I minister not for results, but because I am called.

Perhaps you have similar frustrations about some aspect of your Christian experience. Things haven't turned out the way you thought they would. Sometimes you wonder whether it would be easier just to give up and go with the flow of the world around you.

The Christian life has been described as "a long obedience in the same direction." We must keep on believing day in and day out for years. Yet we can only keep going if we develop an important part of patience—perseverance. James 5 helps us understand that vital quality.

1. In what area of life have you been tempted to "give up"?

2. Read James 5:7–12. What three examples of perseverance does James give?

3. What can the farmer teach us about the value of patience (v. 7)?

4. What might cause us to grumble against each other (v. 9) as we wait for the Lord's return?

5. What happens to fellowship among believers when they grumble against each other?

6. How does the warning that "the Judge is standing at the door" (v. 9) address the problem of grumbling?

7. Three times in verses 7–9 James refers to the Lord's coming. Why does James see it as so important for perseverance?

How does the Lord's return affect your perspective on life?

8. The prophets (v. 10) are an example of patience in suffering, especially since few ever saw any results from their ministry. How do you think they could keep going when God's people rejected their message?

9. Job is also an illustration of patience (v. 11). When he faced severe suffering, his friends weren't good comforters. How can friends sometimes increase the pain of suffering?

How can friends give us strength to persevere in suffering?

10. Another reason to be patient is because of the Lord's compassion and mercy (v. 11). How can these aspects of the Lord's character give you strength to keep going?

11. James gives a severe warning against swearing—taking an oath to guarantee the truth of what you say (v. 12). Why does swearing bring God's condemnation (v. 12; see also Matt. 5:33–37)?

12. Look again at the entire passage. Summarize why perseverance is important for us as Christians.

How can James's advice help you grow in your ability to persevere?

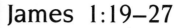

3

The Virtue of Slowness

OCCASIONALLY A DRIVER WOULD swerve around me, casting looks of impatient disgust and a few choice words. I felt bad, but there was little I could do.

We were on a family vacation in a part of the world we had never been to before. Since I didn't know my way around, it was slow going. Looking at road signs and pondering maps takes time. Some drivers behind me were not appreciative.

Living the Christian life can be slow going as well. In fact, the Christian life *should* be slow going. Our initial responses are not always godly ones, and we need to carefully consider our actions and seek the Lord's guidance.

1. How do you respond when others around you don't seem to know what they are doing and get in your way?

2. Read James 1:19–27. The three paragraphs included in these verses are very closely connected but don't necessarily appear to be at first glance. To help you get an overview of the passage, give a brief title to each one (vv. 19–21, 22–25, 26–27).

3. In verse 19, being slow to speak and slow to anger are an important part of a righteous life. How do you think "quick listening" can slow us down and help us to live righteously?

4. Recall a time when you spoke too quickly. Was it related to anger?

   What consequences did it have in your life?

5. Hasty talk and anger are often expressions of worldliness still in our hearts. How can we get rid of moral filth and evil (v. 21)?

6. Getting rid of moral filth and evil requires that we accept the word (v. 21). If the word is already implanted in us, why do we need to humbly accept it?

7. "Slow" action doesn't mean no action. What is the proper approach to God's Word according to verses 22–25?

8. Self-identity is a major issue in counseling today. How can Scripture affect our sense of identity (vv. 23–25)?

9. In our culture there is a tendency to think of law as inhibiting, yet James describes Scripture as the perfect *law* that gives freedom (v. 25). How can God's law give freedom?

10. Twice James warns against self deception (vv. 22, 26). How would you define self-deception?

We can deceive ourselves by forgetfulness, listening without doing, or undisciplined talking. Which kind of deception are you most prone to?

11. Read verses 26–27. Which of the three marks of godly religious behavior mentioned here do you find in your life?

What can you do about the areas where you are weakest?

12. How can you slow down the pace of your life so that you can listen properly to God's Word?

4

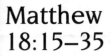

Patience &
Forgiveness

A QUIET DISAGREEMENT DEVELOPED between Mike and me. And it grew.

I was never sure what it was about. I approached him about it once, but he said everything was fine, no problems. So I let it go, and it festered under the surface, occasionally breaking into subtle power struggles in our leadership meetings.

I should have approached him again, but I moved before I got around to it. I was glad to let it go—until I got a letter from a mutual friend. He called me to account, saying that the division between Mike and me was not pleasing to God. He still sensed, even over the thousands of miles, an underlying hostility on both sides. He was right.

So I wrote a letter to Mike, and he wrote back. "Yes," he said, "I am angry." At that point we began the slow and painful process of reconciliation.

In Matthew 18, Jesus tells us that good relationships require work, a special kind of determination, patience, and mercy.

1. When someone offends you, how do you tend to respond?

2. Read Matthew 18:15–20. When a Christian sins against us, Jesus tells us to "go and show him his fault" (v. 15). Why not just avoid the person who offended us?

3. Why do we sometimes want to avoid the process of confrontation and reconciliation?

4. Initially, why is it important to talk privately with the person, keeping the matter "just between the two of you" (v. 15)?

5. If the person will not listen to you, what is the benefit of taking one or two others with you (v. 16)?

   Why can taking others also be threatening?

6. Why do you think a person is to be treated as a non-Christian if he refuses to listen to the church (v. 17)?

7. How does the presence of Jesus among his people (vv. 18–19) relate to the process of reconciliation?

8. Read verses 21–35. What is the connection between Jesus' teaching on reconciliation and Peter's question about the frequency of forgiveness (v. 21)?

9. What is the difference between forgiving seven times and forgiving seventy-seven times (v. 22)?

10. How does the parable of the king and his servant illustrate God's patience and mercy toward us (vv. 23–27)?

11. After being forgiven his massive debt, why do you think the servant refused to be patient and merciful with his fellow servant (vv. 28–30)?

12. God is the master who has forgiven our massive debt of sin. How does the experience of being forgiven affect you?

13. Because God has forgiven us, Jesus requires that we forgive others (v. 35). What does it mean to forgive them "from your heart"?

14. Think of someone who has offended you or sinned against you. What steps do you need to take to extend heart forgiveness to that person?

5

Waiting for the Lord

I HATE TO WAIT.

Waiting in lines, waiting for a long-expected letter, waiting for a phone call, waiting for important information—they all bother me. Yet such things are merely an inconvenience. In his book *Waiting*, Ben Patterson calls us to look more deeply at the issue of waiting:

"There is another, more acute kind of waiting—the waiting of a childless couple for a child; the waiting of a single person for marriage or whatever is next; the waiting of the chronically ill for health or death; the waiting of the emotionally scarred for peace; the waiting of men and women in dead-end careers for a breakthrough; the waiting of unhappy marriages for relief or redemption or escape; the waiting of students to get on with life; the waiting of the lonely to belong.

"For Christians in these kinds of waitings, the question is 'How long, O Lord?' "*

1. When have you been in a situation where you had to wait for the Lord?

2. Read Psalm 40:1–5. David waited patiently for the Lord's help (v. 1). What is the difference between waiting patiently and waiting impatiently?

3. Why is waiting patiently for the Lord often difficult?

4. David was in a slimy pit and a muddy mire—hardly a place to wait patiently! What do you think he was feeling in such circumstances?

5. What "slimy pits" have caused you to cry out to the Lord?

6. God delivered David from the slimy pit and put his feet on a rock (v. 2). What "rocks" has God provided in response to your prayers?

7. Patient waiting requires trust (vv. 3–4). What does it mean to put your trust in the Lord?

8. When we tell others about God's help (v. 3), their faith and ours is strengthened. How does David's account of God's deliverance strengthen your faith?

9. What can you tell others about God's help in your life so that their faith can be strengthened?

10. Why is there such a strong temptation to look to others for help rather than to God (v. 4)?

    What "gods" are you tempted to look to when you are in trouble?

11. It is important to see God's involvement in the everyday events of life. How does your ability to see God's "wonders" compare to David's (v. 5)?

12. In verse 3 David celebrates God's deliverance with a new song. You may not be a poet or song writer, but you can still worship the Lord with your own new song. Take time now or later to write out a few lines of praise to God.

*Ben Patterson, _Waiting: Finding Hope When God Seems Silent_, (Downers Grove, Ill.: InterVarsity Press, 1989) 9–10.

6

Waiting Until
the End

IN TWO MONTHS WE HOPE TO . . ." "In a year we
hope that . . ." Hope for the future. Without it, we give up. With it, we
keep going.

Hope for a vacation can keep us going when pressures at work
become a heavy burden. If we can't see any break in the job, we may
conclude it is better just to quit. Hope for a cure can provide
strength to face an otherwise intolerable level of pain. Pain that
seems endless crushes any desire to go on living.

We all need hope. But hope for next year or even ten years ahead
is not enough. We need a far greater hope for the future. The Apostle
Paul writes of such a hope in the concluding portion of Romans 8.

1. What are some of the things that you hope for?

2. Read Romans 8:18–27. Paul writes that present sufferings are nothing compared to our hope of future glory. Consider the phrases *subjected to frustration* and *bondage to decay* (vv. 20–21). What type of world do they describe?

3. Why do you think Paul places such emphasis on the physical world being restored (vv. 18–21) before talking about the future benefits of our salvation (vv. 22–25)?

4. How would thinking about your troubles as birth pangs (v. 22) affect the way you view them?

5. What do the "family" words Paul uses, like *sons of God* (v. 19), *children of God* (v. 21), *childbirth* (v. 22), and *adoption as sons* (v. 23) convey about our present and future as Christians?

6. How has the Christian family been a help to you in facing hard times?

7. Although we are already God's children (v. 16), what experiences still await us (v. 23)?

8. What causes you to "groan" (v. 23) as you wait for God to complete his work in your life?

9. Hope is central to the Christian faith (vv. 24–25). From these verses, how would you define Christian hope?

10. How is it possible to wait both eagerly (v. 23) and patiently (v. 25) for our hopes to be fulfilled?

11. As we wait, how does the Holy Spirit help us with our weakness and groaning (vv. 26–27)?

12. How does it help you to know that the Spirit is praying for you during your struggles?

13. Thank God for the hope we have in Christ. Ask him for the grace to wait for that hope with eagerness and patience.

Leader's Notes

LEADING A BIBLE DISCUSSION—especially for the first time—can make you feel both nervous and excited. If you are nervous, realize that you are in good company. Many biblical leaders, such as Moses, Joshua, and the apostle Paul, felt nervous and inadequate to lead others (see, for example, 1 Cor. 2:3). Yet God's grace was sufficient for them, just as it will be for you.

Some excitement is also natural. Your leadership is a gift to the others in the group. Keep in mind, however, that other group members also share responsibility for the group. Your role is simply to stimulate discussion by asking questions and encouraging people to respond. The suggestions listed below can help you to be an effective leader.

Preparing to Lead

1. Ask God to help you understand and apply the passage to your own life. Unless that happens, you will not be prepared to lead others.

2. Carefully work through each question in the study guide. Meditate and reflect on the passage as you formulate your answers.

3. Familiarize yourself with the leader's notes for the study. These will help you understand the purpose of the study and will provide valuable information about the questions in the study.

4. Pray for the various members of the group. Ask God to use these studies to bring about greater spiritual fruit in the life of each person.

5. Before the first meeting, make sure each person has a study guide. Encourage them to prepare beforehand for each study.

Leading the Study

1. Begin the study on time. If people realize that the study begins on schedule, they will work harder to arrive on time.

2. At the beginning of your first time together, explain that these studies are designed to be discussions not lectures. Encourage everyone to participate, but realize that some may be hesitant to speak during the first few sessions.

3. Read the introductory paragraph at the beginning of the discussion. This will orient the group to the passage being studied.

4. Read the passage aloud. You may choose to do this yourself, or you might ask for volunteers.

5. The questions in the guide are designed to be used just as they are written. If you wish, you may simply read each one aloud to the group. Or you may prefer to express them in your own words. However, unnecessary rewording of the questions is not recommended.

6. Don't be afraid of silence. People in the group may need time to think before responding.

7. Avoid answering your own questions. If necessary, rephrase a question until it is clearly understood. Even an eager group will quickly become passive and silent if they think the leader will do most of the talking.

8. Encourage more than one answer to each question. Ask, "What do the rest of you think?" or "Anyone else?" until several people have had a chance to respond.

9. Try to be affirming whenever possible. Let people know you appreciate their insights into the passage.

10. Never reject an answer. If it is clearly wrong, ask, "Which verse led you to that conclusion?" Or let the group handle the problem by asking them what they think about the question.

11. Avoid going off on tangents. If people wander off course, gently bring them back to the passage being considered.

12. Conclude your time together with conversational prayer. Ask God to help you apply those things that you learned in the study.

13. End on time. This will be easier if you control the pace of the discussion by not spending too much time on some questions or too little on others.

Many more suggestions and helps are found in the book _Leading Bible Discussions_ (InterVarsity Press). Reading that would be well worth your time.

STUDY 1
The Benefits of Patience
Proverbs 14:29; 15:18; 16:32; 19:11; 25:15

Purpose: To consider how patience can provide many benefits for our lives.

Question 1. Every study begins with an "approach question," which is discussed _before_ reading the passage. An approach question is designed to do three things.

First, it helps to break the ice. Because an approach question doesn't require any knowledge of the passage or any special preparation, it can get people talking and can help them to warm up to each other.

Second, an approach question can motivate people to study the passage at hand. At the beginning of the study, people in the group aren't necessarily ready to jump into the world of the Bible. Their minds may be on other things (their kids, a problem at work, an upcoming meeting) that have nothing to do with the study. An approach question can capture their interest and draw them into the discussion by raising important issues related to the study. The question becomes a bridge between their personal lives and the answers found in Scripture.

Third, a good approach question can reveal where people's thoughts or feelings need to be transformed by Scripture. That is why it is important to ask the approach question *before* reading the passage. The passage might inhibit the spontaneous, honest answers people might have given, because they feel compelled to give biblical answers. The approach question allows them to compare their personal thoughts and feelings with what they later discover in Scripture.

Allow time for this question as it sets up the rest of this study and the ones to follow.

Question 4. Encourage people to be specific. Again, give people time to share.

Question 8. This may be a parent or a teacher. More than likely people will discover that this patient person was one of the most significant people in their lives.

Question 10. These are key distinctions. We may think of a patient person as passive and powerless. Nothing could be further from the truth. Our Lord is the best illustration of true patience. He was neither passive nor powerless.

STUDY 2
The Blessings of Perseverance
James 5:7–12

Purpose: To realize the value of perseverance when we face difficult circumstances, when we are hurting, or when we feel deserted.

Question 2. James is writing to Christians who are experiencing difficulties and disappointments in their faith. In such times it is hard to keep going. The crucial needs and desires of life are beyond our control.

The farmer (v. 7) must wait for the seasons. Rain is scarce in Israel and comes only in the autumn and spring. If a drought comes during those seasons, the farmer's crops are wiped out for the year.

The prophets (v. 10) called Israel to return to the Lord and warned of the consequences if God was spurned. None of the prophets saw the final results of his ministry.

Job's (v. 11) entire family was wiped out in a time of trial. However, he was restored to a life of peace after his time of testing.

Questions 4–6. Verse 9 shows how important and practical the return of the Lord is for everyday living. If we have a sense of impending accountability to God, then even when we lose patience we will put forth the extra effort required.

Question 7. The Lord's coming is referred to in verses 7, 8, and 9 ("the Judge is standing at the door"). If we are to keep going, we need to know that there is an end to our frustrations.

Question 8. The primary reason for perseverance is simply obedience. We are to keep on going in our life and ministry because God has commanded us to.

Question 10. If we fear that in the end we will be condemned, we will give up now. But if we know that mercy awaits us, then we can keep going.

Question 11. D. A. Carson writes: "A sophisticated casuistry judged how binding an oath really was by examining how closely it was related to Yahweh's name. Incredible distinctions proliferate under such an approach. Swearing by heaven and earth was not binding, nor was swearing *by* Jerusalem, though swearing *toward* Jerusalem was. . . . Many groups (e.g., Anabaptists, Jehovah's Witnesses) have understood these verses absolutely literally and have therefore refused even to take court oaths. Their zeal to conform to Scripture is commendable, but they have probably not interpreted the text very well. . . . The contextual purpose of this passage is to stress the true direction in which the OT points—viz., the importance of truthfulness. Where oaths are not being used evasively and truthfulness is not being threatened, it is not immediately obvious that they require such unqualified abolition" (*Matthew*, The Expositor's Bible Commentary [Grand Rapids, Mich.: Zondervan, 1984], 153–54).

STUDY 3
The Virtue of Slowness
James 1:19–27

Purpose: To consider the virtue of being quick to hear, slow to speak, and slow to anger. To grasp the vital importance of not only hearing but doing God's Word.

Question 2. James addresses speaking, righteous living, and turning from the world in the first paragraph and picks on those same issues in the third as well. The central paragraph is the key and addresses all those issues.

Question 5. The Greek word for "moral filth" can also be translated as "impurity." It means having mixed motives, some from the world and some from Scripture. James calls us to get rid of our worldly impurities.

Question 6. God's word is not automatic. We must choose to obey what he has given to us and placed in us.

Question 7. This is a key question for the study. Encourage lots of discussion. The Greek word for *listener* can also be translated as "auditor." James does not want us to be like someone sitting in an auditorium and being entertained by a speaker. Rather, we are to listen to the Word and study it. The Greek word translated as "look intently" can also mean "to stoop down and to look in," as in looking into the bottom of a pond.

Question 8. Only by reading Scripture can we learn what it means to be a Christian. Amid the relentless pressure of a fallen world, it is easy to forget who we are. Our self-identity must be constantly refreshed by God's Word.

Question 9. The idea of law is very biblical but not very modern. In a relativistic age, law is seen as an infringement of personal rights and a restriction of personal self-realization. In the Old Testament the Law was seen as a gift from God to guide us in the right and healthy way of life (see Psalm 119).

Question 10. James used two words for *deception*. The one in verse 22 means to "talk around" the truth. The one in verse 26 means to "walk around" the truth. He also implies a third way of deception, forgetfulness. We simply forget to do the truth. Self deception is very dangerous because we are usually blind to our deception. James exposes our blindness by calling us to look at our actions.

Question 11. The three marks of godly behavior are (1) keeping a tight rein on your tongue, (2) looking after orphans and widows, and (3) avoiding being polluted by the world.

STUDY 4
Patience & Forgiveness
Matthew 18:15–35

Purpose: To discover the relationship between reconciliation, forgiveness, and patience.

Question 2. We are not to avoid each other. Jesus commands us to love one another: "A new command I give you: Love one another. As I have loved you, so you must love one another" (John 13:34–35). This command requires us to embrace others who follow Jesus, even if it is uncomfortable.

Question 3. In many ways it is easier to get angry and reject someone than to seek reconciliation. First, we must go to the person and explain the problem; then we need to ask for an apology. If that fails, Jesus expects us to ask Christian friends to go with us to see the person. If the person still refuses to listen, then we must bring the matter before the entire church. The entire process is difficult and sometimes painful, requiring a great deal of time and effort.

Question 5. Following Christ is not a solitary act; we are joined with each other. When we go with others, they can help us and the other person to see things from a different angle. They may even discover areas where we need to apologize.

Telling people they owe us an apology can be threatening—for us as well as for them. For one thing, confrontation doesn't always bring a positive response on the other person's part. For another, we can appear to be self-righteous and snobbish to the other person. (Which may, in fact, be true.)

Question 6. Jesus places a high priority on the church. We are to work and struggle to get along. But if offenders spurn the advice of the church, they are cutting themselves off not only from the church but from God as well.

Question 7. "These two verses should not in this setting be taken as a promise regarding any prayer on which two or three believers agree (v. 20). . . . The promise is that if two individuals in the church come to agreement concerning any claim they are pursuing (presumably on the basis of the church's judgment, v. 18), 'it will be allowed, ratified (literally it shall succeed, 'come off') on the part of my heavenly Father' . . . This is because God's will and purpose stand behind the binding and loosing of v. 18 and also because ('for,' v. 20) the presence of Jesus is assured with the two or three who are (lit.) 'brought together'—judges solemnly convened before the church and by the church to render a decision. It is a truism of the biblical revelation that God's presence stands with the judges of his people (Ps. 82:1)" (Carson, *Matthew*, 403–04).

According to Jesus, reconciliation requires more than patience and forgiveness. Mercy has no meaning without authority and justice. This can be hard for us to understand in a relativistic society that is blind to moral absolutes. Our culture thinks justice and forgiveness are easy. As Christians we can think that way as well, forgetting the price Christ paid to forgive us and the requirement of repentance that he places on all who enter the kingdom of heaven.

Question 8. Peter understands that forgiveness is important to Jesus. He picks up the theme of forgiveness from the preceding paragraph.

Question 9. Peter thinks he is being gracious by extending forgiveness seven times. Jesus' answer goes far beyond Peter's limited thinking by requiring forgiveness seventy-seven times. The Greek could be translated seven times seventy, essentially an unlimited number.

There is a great difference between limited and unlimited forgiveness. Even if we forgive as many as seven times, we are still counting to see when the limit is reached. Unlimited forgiveness does not keep track of the number of offenses. And this is exactly the forgiveness that God extends to us in Jesus Christ.

Question 10. Being confronted with our sin can produce a repentant heart and a painful awareness that we were wrong. Or being confronted with our wrong-doing can make us angry and determined to be more clever next time. It appears that the latter was the case with the unmerciful servant.

Question 11. The unmerciful servant appears to be upset about being caught in debt and is determined that he won't be in such an uncompromising situation again. Instead, he could have focused on how great was the forgiveness extended to him. And out of gratitude he could have passed that forgiveness on to others.

Question 14. Prayer is very important here, for ourselves and for those we forgive. Forgiveness from the heart requires more than a superficial "I forgive you." We need grace from the Holy Spirit, especially when our hearts seem hesitant to forgive. We must ask God to help us forgive even as we have been forgiven.

STUDY 5
Waiting for the Lord
Psalm 40:1–5

Purpose: To learn to trust the Lord in times of trouble and to look for his help.

This study requires a good bit of vulnerability. How well it goes will depend on the level of trust that has grown up during the time your study group has met. Encourage people to be open about ways God has met some deep needs. But don't pry or push people to share more than they are willing.

At the end of the study there is an optional time of creative writing. If you wish, allow ten minutes or so for that.

Question 2. My dictionary defines *impatience* as "not willing to put up with delay." Another definition is "annoyance." When we wait patiently, we know that the delay has meaning and purpose to it; we choose not to be annoyed. When we wait impatiently, we demonstrate a lack of respect and a lack of trust that God will indeed come through, and we are not willing to put up with it.

Notice, however, that although David waits patiently (v. 1), he also asks the Lord not to delay (v. 17). His request for speedy deliverance is not the same as impatience. There is nothing wrong with asking the Lord to come quickly to our rescue. Yet if he fails to do so, and we become angry and bitter, that is an expression of impatience.

Question 3. When we are facing a difficult situation, it often feels like the Lord is absent or uncaring. This is, of course, not true, but it can feel like it is.

Question 6. God and the Scriptures are our rocks of faith. We can trust that God will help us because the Scriptures say so. But coming to stand on these rocks in times of trouble is not always easy. In a secondary sense, a rock may be a job after a period of joblessness, or a friend after a time of loneliness if we see God as their source and view them as a means of his grace. Otherwise, in time these "solutions" to our needs can also become troublesome muddy pits.

Question 7. This type of trust is more than mere intellectual or abstract believing. It is a confidence that God will be dependable in dangerous situations. It is a confidence that is willing to risk. Analogies might be trusting a guide to get you through an unknown forest; trusting a pilot to fly a plane; trusting a broker to invest your money.

We trust the Lord for our eternal life beyond sin and death. We must also trust him for daily bread and life-crises that we face. A good way to tell how well we trust him to save us from eternal death is to evaluate how much we trust him to help us in the painful events of our daily lives.

Allow the group to ramble a bit here. Let people have lots of freedom to talk about their experiences with God. Everyone can benefit from this.

Question 10. For some of us it is a matter of sight. We trust what we can see, and we can see our bank account or a friend who has enough money to lend. Or perhaps it's a matter of anger. We aren't pleased that God has allowed us to stay in the pit as long as he has. "If God won't help me, I will find someone else who can and will." Also, it is a matter of sinful rebellion. As fallen humans, we would prefer to trust someone other than God.

Gods are not necessarily ancient idols in temples. Anything we trust for deliverance becomes a god to us.

Question 12. If you leave time at the end of the study, this exercise could be a rich experience. Perhaps you could have people write out the first 5 verses of Psalm 40 in their own words. Then ask them to share what they have written.

STUDY 6
Waiting Until the End
Romans 8:18–27

Purpose. To realize that looking forward to the final day of redemption can give us strength to face our present struggles.

This can be a comforting study as well as a painful one. It needs to be lead with sensitivity. As in the last study, the depth of sharing will be determined by how long your Bible study group has been together and how much trust has been built between group members.

Question 2. Encourage people to be honest, but don't probe if they are reticent to share.

Question 3. We are intimately connected with this world in which we live. Before we can ever experience release from sin, the world must be restored.

The Christian faith regards the physical as important. God is the maker of heaven and earth, the visible and the invisible. Further, this world is where we have been placed by God.

Question 4. If we know that our pains are not signs of failure and death, then they can be reminders and aids of the new life that is coming.

Question 5. Death and decay of this present age create terrible separation and loneliness. But in the coming age we will be part of an eternal family where there is only love, forever.

Question 6. Comfort in the face of pain comes from sharing our pain with those who love us.

Question 7. "Adoption was common among the Greeks and Romans, who granted the adopted son all the privileges of a natural son, including inheritance rights . . . Christians are already God's children, but this is a reference to the full realization of our inheritance in Christ" (*The* NIV *Study Bible* [Grand Rapids, Mich.: Zondervan, 1985], notes to Rom. 8:15, 23). The resurrection is the final stage in our adoption.

Notice, too, Paul's reference to "the firstfruits of the Spirit" (v. 23). Like the firstfruits of a harvest, the Holy Spirit is a pledge of more and greater things to come. Likewise, he is a down payment of our future inheritance.

Questions 11–12. The present age for Christians is not free of pain (vv. 23, 26). In fact, while having the Spirit removes us from the power of sin, it also puts us into a struggle with sin, a struggle that can lead to inward groaning. However, the Spirit helps us in our groaning and weakness by bringing our needs before God.

Question 13. We can wait eagerly for our hope because we know it is coming. We can wait patiently because we trust that God is active now and is working to bring about that final day in his own good time.